TOP 10 BASEBALL HITTERS

Bill Deane

SPORTS TOP 10

Enslow Publishers, Inc.

44 Fadem Road   PO Box 38
Box 699   Aldershot
Springfield, NJ 07081   Hants GU12 6BP
USA   UK

Dedication

To Gig, #1 on the list of Top 10 Friends

Acknowledgments

The author wishes to thank Bryan Reilly (PF Sports Images), Mark Rucker (Transcendental Graphics), and Dana Wickes for their help in providing the photographs for this book; Tim Wiles, Scot Mondore, Bruce Markusen, and Dan Bennett of the National Baseball Library & Archive, for their research assistance; and Sarah Deane, for her expert editorial help and advice.

Library of Congress Cataloging-in-Publication Data

Deane, Bill.
     Top 10 baseball hitters / Bill Deane.
         p. cm. — (Sports top 10)
     Includes bibliographical references (p.) and index.
     Summary: Profiles the lives and careers of Hank Aaron, Ty Cobb, Tony Gwynn, Rogers Hornsby, Stan Musial, Pete Rose, Babe Ruth, Frank Thomas, Honus Wagner, and Ted Williams.
     ISBN 0-7660-1007-4
     1. Baseball players—United States—Biography—Juvenile literature.
     2. Baseball players—Rating of—United States—Juvenile literature. 3. Batting (Baseball)—Juvenile literature. [1. Baseball players.] I. Title. II. Series.
GV865.A1D372 1998
796.357'26'092273—dc21
[B]   97-21633
                                         CIP
                                         AC

Printed in the United States of America

10 9 8 7 6 5 4 3 2 1

Illustration Credits: Bill Deane, p. 26; PF Sports Images, Yonkers, NY, pp. 7, 9, 10, 14, 17, 23, 25, 30, 34, 37, 42, 45; Photo by Dana C. Wickes, p. 29; Transcendental Graphics, Boulder, CO, pp. 13, 18, 21, 33, 39, 41.

Cover Illustration: PF Sports Images, Yonkers, NY.

Interior Design: Richard Stalzer

CONTENTS

INTRODUCTION

WHAT MAKES A GREAT HITTER? Is it someone who hits for a high batting average by slapping the ball to all fields, or someone who swings for power and drives in a lot of runs? Is it someone who is patient, not swinging at any balls out of the strike zone, or someone who goes up to the plate hacking away?

Great hitters do all of these things, depending on the situation. If a team needs to start a rally, a great hitter will be patient, looking for a single or a walk to reach base. If a team has runners on base, a great hitter will look for a pitch he can hit hard enough to score the runners. One of the best-known statistics for rating hitters is batting average, the average number of hits per time at bat. A batting average of .300 or better is considered the magic number for great hitters.

This book profiles our choices for the ten best hitters in baseball history. In selecting them, we looked first at total hits, career batting average, and league leaderships in that category. But batting average is not the only important measure of a hitter's skill. We also paid attention to on-base percentage (OBP) and slugging percentage (SLG). OBP is the percentage of times a player reaches base on hits, walks, and being hit by pitches. SLG is the average number of total bases made by a hitter per time at bat. If a player can maintain averages of .300 (batting), .350 (OBP), and .450 (SLG), he will rank among the very best all-around hitters in the game.

In cutting the list down to ten, we had to omit many great hitters. These include Shoeless Joe Jackson, Tris Speaker,

Lou Gehrig, Willie Mays, Rod Carew, and Negro Leagues stars Josh Gibson and Oscar Charleston.

It's hard to go wrong with the ten selections we did make. These are the players that fans love—and pitchers hate—to see come up in a crucial moment of the game.

CAREER STATISTICS

Player	YR	G	AB	R	H	AVG	LL	OBP	SLG
HANK AARON	23	3,298	12,364	2,174	3,771	.305	2	.377	.555
TY COBB	24	3,035	11,434	2,246	4,189	.366	12	.433	.512
TONY GWYNN	15	1,946	7,595	1,140	2,560	.337	7	.391	.448
ROGERS HORNSBY	23	2,259	8,173	1,579	2,930	.358	7	.434	.577
STAN MUSIAL	22	3,026	10,972	1,949	3,630	.331	7	.418	.559
PETE ROSE	24	3,562	14,053	2,165	4,256	.303	3	.377	.409
BABE RUTH	22	2,503	8,399	2,174	2,873	.342	1	.474	.690
FRANK THOMAS	7	930	3,291	675	1,077	.327	0	.456	.599
HONUS WAGNER	21	2,792	10,430	1,736	3,415	.327	8	.391	.466
TED WILLIAMS	19	2,292	7,706	1,798	2,654	.344	6	.483	.634

KEY:

YR = years in majors
G = games played
AB = times at bat

R = runs scored
H = hits
AVG = batting average

LL = league batting leaderships
OBP = on-base percentage
SLG = slugging percentage

HANK AARON

IN 1968 HANK AARON HIT 29 homers, drove in 87 runs, and batted .287. These are good numbers for most players, but for Aaron they were disappointing. After all, Aaron had averaged 36 homers, 113 RBI, and a .318 average each year over the previous thirteen seasons. Some people thought maybe Father Time had finally caught up with him at age thirty-four.

But Aaron didn't think so. In 1969, he came back to bat .300, hit 44 home runs, and lead his team to the divisional title. Two years later, he hit .327 with a career-high 47 home runs. At age thirty-nine, Aaron batted .301 with 40 homers. "I take pride in what I'm doing every day I go out there," said Aaron. "I know there will be bad days and bad games, but I want to be consistent."[1]

Henry Louis Aaron was born on February 5, 1934. He had seven brothers and sisters. His brother Tommie would also play in the big leagues one day. In his birthplace of Mobile, Alabama, Henry attended Central High School before graduating from Josephine Allen Institute. Although neither school had a baseball team, he had become an outstanding ballplayer in local leagues. He joined the Indianapolis Clowns, a Negro League team, and soon was noticed by big league scouts. Aaron then signed with the Braves' organization, and batted .353 in the minor leagues.

By age twenty, Aaron was in the majors. Though he was not a large man, the right-handed batter had strong forearms and quick wrists. This meant that he could wait a little longer than most hitters before deciding whether or not to

HANK AARON

Following through on his swing, Hank Aaron connects on another deep smash. Aaron always played his best when it mattered the most. His career batting average in World Series play is .364.

swing. When you are facing 90-mile-per-hour pitches, every split second counts!

Aaron soon became one of the best and most consistent players in the game, having one great year after another. In 1956 he won the NL batting title and the Player of the Year Award. A year later, he led the Braves to the world championship and was named the league's MVP. In 1959 Hammerin' Hank hit .355 to win another batting title. In 1963, he won another Player of the Year Award. Aaron hit line drives to all fields, many of them going for doubles, triples, or home runs. He also won three Gold Glove Awards for excellence in the outfield, and became one of the league's best base-stealers. But, because he wasn't loud or flashy, people hardly noticed Aaron's performances.

Late in his career, Aaron's lifetime statistics were really piling up. It was only then that people realized what a great player he had been and still was. In 1968, he became just the eighth player to reach 500 career home runs. Two years later, he became the ninth to reach 3,000 hits. In 1972, he got his 2,000th RBI, something only Babe Ruth had done before. But it was in 1974, when he broke Ruth's career home run record—once thought unbeatable—that Aaron's legend was complete. He wound up with 755 homers, and also set records for most career extra-base hits, total bases, and runs batted in.

Most baseball fans know about Aaron's home run record, but few remember what a great all-around player he was. "As far as I'm concerned, Aaron is the best ballplayer of my era," said Hall of Famer Mickey Mantle. "He's never received the credit he's due."[2]

HANK AARON

BORN: February 5, 1934, Mobile, Alabama.

HIGH SCHOOL: Central High School and Josephine Allen Institute, Mobile, Alabama.

PRO: Milwaukee Braves, 1954–1965; Atlanta Braves, 1966–1974; Milwaukee Brewers, 1975–1976.

RECORDS: Most home runs, 755; Most runs batted in, 2,297; Most extra-base hits, 1,477; Most total bases on hits, 6,856.

HONORS: NL MVP, 1957; NL Player of the Year, 1956, 1963; Gold Glove Award, 1958–1960; Elected to National Baseball Hall of Fame, 1982.

In addition to his awesome batting statistics, Aaron was also solid in the field. He received the Gold Glove Award in three consecutive seasons.

TY COBB

Ty Cobb was one of the most exciting players in baseball history. Cobb won the Triple Crown in 1909 by leading the league in batting average (.377), home runs (9), and RBI (107).

AS THE BASEBALL HALL OF FAME prepared for its very first election in 1936, many people wondered how well Ty Cobb would do. Although Cobb was a tremendous player, he was also an unpleasant, sometimes vicious man. He was hated by players, writers, and followers of the game. The election might be the writers' chance to get even with Cobb by not voting for him.

But the writers could not ignore what Cobb had accomplished on the diamond. When the votes were in, Cobb had been named on 98 percent of the ballots—more than anybody else. "In any all-time rating of players, Tyrus Raymond Cobb stands alone," said one writer. "He was the greatest of the great."[1]

Ty Cobb was born on December 18, 1886, in Narrows, Georgia, and grew up in nearby Royston. His father, a state senator, wanted Ty to become a lawyer or doctor, but the youngster had other ideas. At age seventeen, he left to become a professional ballplayer. "Don't come home a failure," his father warned him.[2]

Cobb devoted the next twenty-five years to becoming the best player he could possibly be. After a shaky first year in the minors, the outfielder led his league in batting in 1905. The Detroit Tigers signed him before the season was over.

Cobb had an odd way of hitting. The lefty swinger stood with his feet close together, used a large bat, and held his hands several inches apart on the handle. When he wanted to swing for a base hit, he would move his bottom hand up as the pitch came. When he wanted to swing for power, he would move the top hand down.

Strange as it may have been, it worked for Cobb. In 1907, at age twenty, he won his first American League batting title. Then he won another title, and another—nine straight batting crowns in all! Along the way, he led the Tigers to three pennants in a row, and won the Triple Crown in 1909. But his best year was in 1911, when he batted an amazing .420, leading the league in runs (147), hits (248), doubles (47), triples (24), RBI (127), and stolen bases (83).

Even these awesome numbers don't tell how Cobb could take over a game all by himself. On May 12, 1911, for example, Cobb scored all the way from first base on a short single in one inning, and scored from second base on a wild pitch in another. To cap off the day, he stole home with the winning run in a 6–5 victory. On May 5, 1925, after criticism that he was not enough of a power hitter, Cobb said, "I'll show you something today—I'm going for home runs for the first time in my career."[3] That day, the thirty-eight-year-old Cobb collected three homers, a double, and two singles in a 14–8 Tigers win. The next day, he hit two more homers. It seemed as if Cobb could do anything he wanted on a ballfield.

Cobb won twelve batting championships in all, a record nobody has come close to. His .366 lifetime batting average also stands safely atop the list. These were among dozens of records Cobb left behind when he finally retired in 1928. Some have been broken, but many people still consider Cobb the greatest, fiercest competitor the game has ever known.

TY COBB

BORN: December 18, 1886, Narrows, Georgia.

DIED: July 17, 1961, Atlanta, Georgia.

HIGH SCHOOL: Franklin County Comprehensive High School, Royston, Georgia.

PRO: Detroit Tigers, 1905–1926; Philadelphia Athletics, 1927–1928.

RECORDS: Highest batting average, career (.366); Most runs scored (2,246); Most years (12) and most consecutive years (9) leading league in batting average.

HONORS: AL Chalmers (MVP) Award, 1911; Triple Crown, 1909; Elected to National Baseball Hall of Fame, 1936.

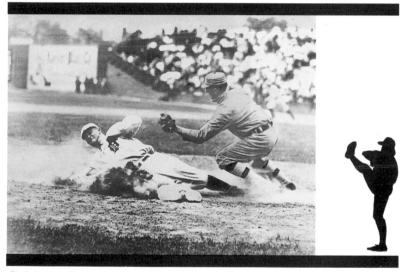

Cobb is forced to slide after making another daring base running move. He led the American League in stolen bases six times during his career.

TONY GWYNN

Tony Gwynn reaches down to get a pitch low in the strike zone. An excellent athlete, Gwynn was even drafted by the San Diego Clippers to play professional basketball.

TONY GWYNN

TONY GWYNN WAS TRYING to do something that hadn't been done since 1952: win three straight National League batting titles. With two games left in the 1989 season, the Giants' Will Clark was ahead of Gwynn, .334 to .331. To add to the drama, the two players would be playing against each other in those two games.

Clark did all right, going 2-for-8 to finish with a solid .333 average. But Gwynn blasted out six hits in eight tries to win the title at .336. "He is simply amazing," said one-time teammate Joe Carter about Gwynn. "You just never expect him to make an out."[1]

Anthony Keith Gwynn was born May 9, 1960, in Los Angeles, California. As a youngster, he would play baseball all day long with his two older brothers, using homemade balls. By age thirteen, Tony was good enough to play on an adults' team. His best sport, however, was basketball. After graduating from Long Beach Polytechnic High School, Gwynn went to San Diego State to play college hoops. Although he stood just 5 feet 11 inches, he set the school's all-time record for assists, and was chosen by the San Diego Clippers in the 1981 National Basketball Association draft.

Gwynn was selected by the San Diego Padres in baseball's free agent draft that very same week. Now he had a choice to make: pro basketball or baseball? He decided he had a better, longer future in baseball, and he started his minor-league career almost immediately.

Within thirteen months, Gwynn climbed all the way from Class A to the major leagues, but he broke both wrists within a half-year of his big-league debut. The injuries cost him months of playing time, and Gwynn was able to play in only 140 games over his first two seasons with the Padres. Still, he batted over .300, and had the majors' longest hitting streak of 1983.

Gwynn finally got a chance to play a full season in 1984, and he made it count. The outfielder topped the NL in hits, batting average (.351), and on-base percentage, leading the Padres to the league pennant. Gwynn went on to win batting titles in 1987, 1988, and 1989, too. His .370 average in 1987 was the NL's highest since Stan Musial hit .376 in 1948.

Gwynn uses the smallest bat in the major leagues: $32\frac{1}{2}$ inches long, 32 ounces in weight. The lefty crouches near the back of the batter's box and strides into the pitch with an inside-out swing. Tony's wife, Alicia, videotapes every one of his times at bat so he can analyze his swing each day. It is all part of the preparation and hard work that go into being the best hitter in baseball.

In 1994, Gwynn was threatening to become the big leagues' first .400 hitter since Ted Williams, but a player strike ended the season in August. Gwynn finished at .394—still the highest single-season average since 1941. Through 1996, Gwynn had batted over .300 for fourteen straight seasons.

In his midthirties, when most players slow down, Gwynn was at the top of his game. Between 1993 and 1996, he batted a combined .367, winning three more batting titles, for a grand total of seven. "I can honestly say that I would pay to see him hit," said former batting champ Al Oliver. "He has no weaknesses."[2]

TONY GWYNN

BORN: May 9, 1960, Los Angeles, California.

HIGH SCHOOL: Long Beach Polytechnic High School, Long Beach, California.

COLLEGE: San Diego State University, San Diego, California.

PRO: San Diego Padres, 1982– .

HONORS: Gold Glove Award, 1986–1987, 1989–1991.

In 1996 Tony Gwynn won his seventh batting title. Only two players, Ty Cobb, and Honus Wagner have ever won more.

ROGERS HORNSBY

Rogers Hornsby shows off his mighty swing. In 1924, Hornsby batted .424, and no one has hit for a higher average since.

ROGERS HORNSBY

NOBODY COULD HAVE EXPECTED Rogers Hornsby to become a great hitter. He weighed only 135 pounds when he began his big-league career. He was a shortstop, a position that is usually filled by good fielders with weak bats. Hornsby had batted only .255 in the minor leagues, and he hit right-handed, while most great hitters bat left-handed. Lefties finish their swings about two steps closer to first base than righties do.

But Rogers Hornsby overcame all of these handicaps. He wound up winning seven batting titles, and topping the .400 mark three times. Famous sportswriter John Drebinger summed up Hornsby's legacy: "As a batsman, he justly deserved the title as baseball's greatest right-handed hitter."[1]

Rogers Hornsby was born April 27, 1896, in Winters, Texas. The odd first name came from his mother's maiden name, Mary Rogers. Hornsby went to North Side High School in Fort Worth, Texas, before starting his pro baseball career in 1914.

A year later, Hornsby made it to the majors with the St. Louis Cardinals. He stood in the back corner of the batter's box, hitting to all fields with quick reflexes and a level swing. He seemed to have a gift for hitting the ball to places where no fielders were.

Hornsby had more than talent. He was dedicated to physical fitness and to the art of hitting. He got a lot of sleep and stayed away from tobacco and alcohol. He even avoided movies, fearing they would weaken his eyes. Hornsby studied pitchers, learned their weaknesses, and had no mercy for them. "The only emotion or thought I ever had for a pitcher was to feel sorry for him," Hornsby once said.[2]

Hornsby eventually matured from a 135-pound slaphitter into a 200-pound slugger. In 1920, he moved to second base, and won his first batting title with a hearty .370 average. He improved to .397 the next year. And, in 1922, Hornsby won the Triple Crown with 42 homers, 152 RBI, and a .401 average.

After hitting .384 in 1923, Hornsby set a modern record that may never be broken: He batted .424 in 1924. In 1925, he had probably his best offensive season. He hit 39 homers, drove in 143 runs, and batted .403 to win his sixth straight batting title, his second Triple Crown, and the league MVP Award. In the five seasons starting in 1921, Hornsby had averaged an incredible .402! Even a slowpitch softball player would be satisfied with that!

Hornsby became a player-manager, and changed teams three times between 1927 and 1929. He hit well wherever he went: .361 for the Giants, .387 for the Braves, and .380 for the Cubs, with whom he won another MVP Award.

Leg injuries slowed down Hornsby after that. He had surgery on his heel in 1929, broke an ankle sliding in 1930, and injured his thigh in 1931. He played very little over the rest of his career. Hornsby wound up with a .358 lifetime average, second behind only Ty Cobb. He spent much of the rest of his life coaching and working with kids.

Hornsby received the ultimate reward in 1942. As the newspapers put it, "the fabulous baseball career of Rogers Hornsby, the greatest right-handed hitter of all time, carried him into the Hall of Fame."[3]

ROGERS HORNSBY

BORN: April 27, 1896, Winters, Texas.

DIED: January 5, 1963, Chicago, Illinois.

HIGH SCHOOL: North Side High School, Fort Worth, Texas.

PRO: St. Louis Cardinals, 1915–1926, 1933; New York Giants, 1927; Boston Braves, 1928; Chicago Cubs, 1929–1932; St. Louis Browns, 1933–1937.

RECORDS: Highest batting average, season since 1900 (.424 in 1924); Highest batting average, career, NL (.359); Highest slugging percentage, career, NL (.578).

HONORS: Triple Crown, 1922, 1925; NL MVP, 1925, 1929; Elected to National Baseball Hall of Fame, 1942.

In 1926, Hornsby was player-manager of the St. Louis Cardinals and led them to a World Series victory. Hornsby won his second Most Valuable Player award as a member of the Chicago Cubs for his efforts during the 1929 season.

STAN MUSIAL

STAN MUSIAL WAS FORTY-ONE years old and coming off the three worst years of his career. After batting .340 over his first 17 seasons, Musial had averaged just .273 since 1958. He had been benched for weeks at a time, and his pay had been cut by 30 percent. It looked like it was time for him to retire.

But Stan the Man had one big season left. In 1962, Musial broke the National League career records for games played, hits, runs scored, and RBI. He homered in four straight at bats in July, and went 5-for-5 in a late September game. Musial challenged for the league batting title and finished with a robust .330 average. Retirement would have to wait another year.

Stanley Frank Musial was born November 21, 1920, in Donora, Pennsylvania, the same small town that would later produce big-league stars Ken Griffey, Senior and Junior. The son of poor Polish immigrants, Stan graduated from Donora High School, where he played football and basketball in addition to baseball.

Musial began his pro baseball career in 1938 as a pitcher. He won 33 games and lost only 13 over the next three seasons. But he also showed great ability as a hitter, and often was used as an outfielder or pinch hitter when he wasn't pitching. When Musial injured his pitching shoulder in 1940, he was converted into a full-time outfielder. It turned out to be a lucky break for him. He batted .364 in 1941 during a whirlwind rise from Class C to the major leagues. Except for a year in the U.S. Navy, Musial played

STAN MUSIAL

Stan Musial was one of the best players of the 1940s and 1950s. He played in twenty-four All-Star Games.

for the St. Louis Cardinals for the next twenty-two seasons, leading them to four pennants.

Musial had an unusual batting stance. The lefty crouched in the back of the batter's box, with his knees pointing toward each other and his back toward the pitcher. He faced the pitcher as if he were peeking around a corner, and wiggled his body as he awaited the pitch. When Musial saw one he liked, he would uncoil like a snake, snapping the bat forward, and usually driving the ball toward the outfield gap.

Musial had one great season after another. He earned three MVP Awards and finished second another four times. He won seven NL batting titles. His best season came in 1948. That year, Stan led the league in runs (135), hits (230), doubles (46), triples (18), RBI (131), batting (.376), and slugging (.702). He had four five-hit games, a record, and hit 39 home runs, his career high. Had he hit just one more, he would have won the Triple Crown, becoming the only man ever to lead his league in hits, doubles, triples, and homers in the same season!

No matter how well he did, he was always just happy to be a ballplayer. "The biggest thrill I get," he often said, "is putting on that uniform every day, feeling how lucky I am to be getting paid to play the game."[1]

When Musial finally retired in 1963, he had collected 3,630 hits, including 725 doubles, 177 triples, and 475 home runs. "Stan Musial is one of the all-time greats," said Hank Aaron, the man who would later break most of Stan's NL records. "He's the greatest hitter I ever saw."[2]

STAN MUSIAL

BORN: November 21, 1920, Donora, Pennsylvania.

HIGH SCHOOL: Donora High School, Donora, Pennsylvania.

PRO: St. Louis Cardinals, 1941–1944, 1946–1963.

HONORS: NL MVP, 1943, 1946, 1948; NL Player of the Year, 1943, 1946, 1948, 1951, 1957; Major League Player of the Decade, 1956; Elected to National Baseball Hall of Fame, 1969.

Musial started his career as a pitcher and was eventually switched to the outfield after an injury. Brooklyn fans nicknamed him "the Man" because of his success at the Brooklyn Dodgers' Ebbets Field.

PETE ROSE

Known as "Charlie Hustle" because of his hard-nosed style of play, Pete Rose became the all-time leader in hits in 1985.

PETE ROSE

TY COBB HAD RETIRED in 1928 with nearly 4,200 lifetime hits. Nobody before or since had come close. Then came Pete Rose, a player who reminded people of Cobb, for his fierce determination as well as his batting ability. Rose was durable and consistent, collecting around two hundred hits year after year. By September 11, 1985, he needed just one more to break Cobb's record.

On his first time up that night, Rose lined a single to left field. The 47,237 fans gave him a seven-minute ovation. Rose was overcome with emotion, but, true to his nature, he kept playing—and playing to win. He later tripled and walked, scored twice, and made a diving stop at first base to end the game, giving his Reds a 2–0 win.

Peter Edward Rose was born in Cincinnati, Ohio, on April 14, 1941. Starting when Rose was just a little boy, his father and uncle began teaching him to switch-hit and to play hard all the time. Rose was small in size and talent, but big on determination. Pro scout Buddy Bloebaum—Rose's uncle—convinced the Reds to sign the youngster in 1960.

Rose spent three seasons in the minors, growing and improving each year. He batted out of a crouch, watching each pitch from the pitcher's hand to home plate. Rose had great bat control and hand-eye coordination. He especially impressed people with his hustle, stretching singles into doubles and doubles into triples.

Rose was NL Rookie of the Year in 1963. He went on to lead the league in hits seven times, doubles five times, runs four times, and batting three times. In 1978, he hit safely in

44 straight games, an NL record. A year later, he had his tenth 200-hit season, another record.

Rose helped the Reds to become perhaps the greatest team in history. Known as the Big Red Machine, they won world championships in 1975 and 1976. In 1980, after switching teams, Rose led the Phillies to their first world title ever. He batted .381 lifetime in 28 LCS games, and hit .370 to win the 1975 World Series MVP.

Rose's contributions went beyond stats. He often switched positions to make room for future stars like Tony Perez, Lee May, and George Foster. Rose eventually played at six different positions, becoming an All-Star at five of them. And, setting an example by always hustling, he brought out the best in his teammates. As one observer said, "his desire and enthusiasm spread throughout the team."[1] Stars Joe Morgan and Mike Schmidt credit Rose with helping them to become Hall of Famers.

Rose didn't smoke or drink, and he always took good care of himself. This helped him to play more games than anyone else in history. But, by age forty-three, Rose had gone from the Phillies to the Expos and was hardly playing. In a surprise move, Rose returned to Cincinnati to become player-manager. He batted .365 the rest of the 1984 season, setting the stage for his 1985 heroics. Rose finished with 4,256 career hits, a record that will surely last a long, long time.

Because of troubles after his career ended, Rose has not been allowed a place in the Hall of Fame. But, nothing can change what he accomplished on the field. Of the 15,000 players in major-league history, none has more hits than Rose, and none played harder. As great manager Sparky Anderson said, "he is the greatest single competitor I have ever been associated with."[2]

PETE ROSE

Born: April 14, 1941, Cincinnati, Ohio.

High School: Western Hills High School, Cincinnati, Ohio.

Pro: Cincinnati Reds, 1963–1978, 1984–1986; Philadelphia Phillies, 1979–1983; Montreal Expos, 1984.

Records: Most games (3,562); Most hits (4,256); Most runs, NL (2,165); Most years collecting 200 or more hits (10); Most consecutive games, one or more hits, NL (44 in 1978).

Honors: NL Rookie of the Year, 1963; NL Player of the Year, 1968; NL MVP, 1973; Major League Player of the Decade, 1980; Gold Glove Award, 1969–1970.

Rose's opponents knew that he was a dangerous hitter. He could often stretch singles into doubles.

BABE RUTH

Babe Ruth takes some warm-up swings before game
time. Most experts still regard Ruth to be the
greatest slugger the game has ever seen.

AT AGE THIRTY, BABE RUTH wasn't taking care of himself as he should have been. He was eating and drinking too much. He was arguing with his manager and getting into trouble on and off the field. He missed fifty-eight games, and his team slipped from second place to seventh. Many people thought the Sultan of Swat was washed up.

But the Babe got his act together and came back strong. He led the league in home runs and slugging percentage in each of the next six seasons, averaging 50 homers per year. He set a new record with 60 homers in 1927, which was more than any other entire AL team hit that year! In all, he lasted ten more seasons, retiring as the greatest slugger in the game's history.

George Herman Ruth was born February 6, 1895, in Baltimore, Maryland. Because of problems he encountered as a child, he spent twelve years at a Catholic reform school, where he developed his baseball skills. At age nineteen he was noticed by Jack Dunn, owner of Baltimore's minor-league team. Dunn had to become Ruth's legal guardian in order to take him from the school. People started calling the youngster Dunn's Babe.

The Babe soon made it to the major leagues as a pitcher for the Red Sox. He became the best left-hander in the league. He was also an excellent hitter, taking big swings with a huge bat. Some people thought he could win more games for Boston batting every day instead of pitching every four days. The Red Sox eventually converted Ruth into a full-time outfielder.

In 1919, Ruth hit 29 homers, a new major-league record. Sold to the New York Yankees in 1920, he almost doubled that record by smashing 54 homers. A year later, he hit 59. In just three seasons, he had hit more home runs than anyone else had hit in an entire career!

But Ruth was far more than just a home run hitter. Between 1920 and 1931, he averaged .357, topping .370 six times. In 1921, he had the greatest season in big-league history, setting records for the most runs scored (177), extra-base hits (119), and total bases (457) in a year. He batted .393 to win the MVP Award in 1923, and .378 to win the batting title the next year.

Ruth's slugging turned the Yankees into champions, doubling their attendance. This made it possible for the team to build Yankee Stadium, which was called "the House that Ruth Built." It also made Ruth the highest-paid performer in baseball, earning double what any other player made at the time. In 1923, Babe Ruth led the Yanks to their first world championship. He and teammate Lou Gehrig would lead them to three more Series titles, on what many people consider the best team ever.

On May 25, 1935, Ruth hit his final three home runs. That gave him a career total of 714—more than double anybody else's total to that point. His lifetime slugging percentage (.690) is still the best ever, by far. He retired the next week, the most popular and legendary sports figure of all time. Stories about Ruth's records and feats seemed incredible to later fans. "I stopped talking about the Babe," said one writer, "for the simple reason that . . . those who had never seen him didn't believe me."[1]

BABE RUTH

BORN: February 6, 1895, Baltimore, Maryland.

DIED: August 16, 1948, New York, New York.

HIGH SCHOOL: St. Mary's Industrial School for Boys, Baltimore, Maryland.

PRO: Boston Red Sox, 1914–1919; New York Yankees, 1920–1934; Boston Braves, 1935.

RECORDS: Most home runs by left-handed batter, 714; Most years leading league in home runs, 12; Most runs scored, season (177 in 1921); Most bases on balls, season (170 in 1923) and career (2,056); Highest slugging percentage, season (.847 in 1920) and career (.690).

HONORS: AL MVP, 1923; Elected to National Baseball Hall of Fame, 1936.

Babe Ruth appears to be watching one of his 714 career home runs sail out of the yard. Ruth was inducted into the National Baseball Hall of Fame in 1936, the first year elections were held.

FRANK THOMAS

Frank Thomas surveys the damage he just inflicted upon the opposing team. Thomas was originally given a football scholarship to Auburn University.

FRANK THOMAS

FRANK THOMAS WAS VERY DISAPPOINTED. He was hoping to get drafted to play professional baseball right out of high school. But, because of his size (6 feet 5 inches tall, 257 pounds), he was considered more of a football player. Baseball's 1986 Free Agent draft came and went, and not a single team chose him.

In 1989, it was a different story. Thomas had starred in college ball for three years, and made it clear that baseball was his sport of choice. The Chicago White Sox made him the nation's seventh player selected in the draft. He was on his way to becoming the most dangerous hitter in the big leagues.

Frank Edward Thomas, Jr., was born in Columbus, Georgia, on May 27, 1968. Frank starred in football as well as baseball at Columbus High School. After the disappointing baseball draft, he accepted a full football scholarship to Auburn University.

After a 1987 leg injury ended Thomas's football career, he decided to devote his full attention to baseball. He was an all-conference selection in each of his three years at Auburn, setting several school records. He then started his pro career, and was named Minor League Player of the Year in 1990.

Thomas earned the call to the big leagues later that summer, and batted .330 over the last two months of the season. In 1991, his first full year in the Show, he batted .318, leading the league in walks and on-base percentage (OBP). The next year, he again topped the AL in walks and OBP, also leading in doubles. Thomas became known as the Big Hurt, for the pain he caused opposing teams and pitchers.

In 1993, the huge first baseman became the power hitter everyone expected. Thomas smashed 41 homers and drove in 128 runs to lead the Sox to the divisional title. He was even better in 1994. In the strike-shortened season, Thomas batted .353, with 38 homers in 113 games. His .729 slugging percentage and .487 on-base percentage were among the best ever. He was overwhelmingly named MVP in both seasons.

Thomas didn't stop there. In 1995, he hit 40 home runs and led the league in walks and sacrifice flies. In 1996, despite a broken foot, he batted .349 with 40 more homers and 134 RBI.

Some batters hit for high average, others hit for power. The right-handed Thomas is the rare player who does both. He uses an inside-out swing, where his top hand is released from the bat during the follow-through. It is a style usually associated with slap hitters, but it doesn't prevent Thomas from hitting the ball as far as anyone else in the game.

If he can stay healthy over the next ten years or so, Frank Thomas should rank among the all-time greats. Entering the 1997 season, the twenty-nine-year-old Thomas had career averages of .327 (batting), .456 (on-base), and .599 (slugging). Only two players surpass the Big Hurt in all three categories. Perhaps Thomas will join those two—Babe Ruth and Ted Williams—to be considered one of the three most destructive hitters in major league history.

Thomas isn't resting on his laurels. "I'm still a young player," he says. "I'm still learning the game and I'm still having fun. I've still got a lot to prove."[1]

FRANK THOMAS

BORN: May 27, 1968, Columbus, Georgia.

HIGH SCHOOL: Columbus High School, Columbus, Georgia.

COLLEGE: Auburn University, Auburn, Alabama.

PRO: Chicago White Sox, 1990– .

HONORS: AL MVP, 1993, 1994; Major League Player of the Year, 1993.

Thomas watches intently, knowing that the ball might be coming his way. In 1994, he became only the eleventh player to win the MVP award in consecutive seasons.

HONUS WAGNER

IN 1996, A SINGLE BASEBALL CARD was sold for $640,500, by far the most ever paid for a card. What superstar was depicted on this piece of cardboard? Was it the popular 12-time home run champion, Babe Ruth? Or the ferocious 12-time batting champion, Ty Cobb? Was it legendary pitcher Cy Young, winner of more than 500 games? Or Hammerin' Henry Aaron, hitter of more than 750 home runs?

It was none of these greats. The most valuable baseball card depicts a quiet, funny-looking player who started his career a century ago. His name is Honus Wagner.

John Peter Wagner was born in Mansfield, Pennsylvania, on February 24, 1874. He was of German ancestry, and the German name for John is Johannes. This sounded like "Honus" to his childhood friends, and he was known as Honus Wagner from then on. At age twelve, Honus quit school to work with his father in the coal mines. When he wasn't working, he was playing baseball. "Even darkness never fully stopped me," Honus said. "I practiced until I was called to bed."[1]

Honus played semi-pro baseball for several years. His older brother, Al, was on a professional team, and recommended that they sign up the younger Wagner. Honus turned pro in 1895, and joined the National League's Louisville team two years later.

In 1900, the team was dissolved, with fifteen of its players transferring to Pittsburgh. Wagner became a member of the Pirates. He played every position, but eventually found his home at shortstop. Known as the Flying Dutchman,

HONUS WAGNER

Honus Wagner is one of the best all-around players in baseball history. He was an excellent hitter and fielder, and led the National League in stolen bases on five occasions.

Wagner was an excellent fielder and base runner, leading the NL in fielding three times and in stolen bases five times. But hitting was what he did best.

The bowlegged, right-handed Wagner won his first batting title in 1900 with a .381 average. He led the Pirates to NL pennants in each of the next three years, and to the world championship in 1909. Between 1903 and 1909, Wagner won six of a possible seven batting crowns, finishing second in the other year. In 1911, he won his eighth title, a record surpassed only by Ty Cobb. Wagner wasn't just a singles hitter, either. He led the league in doubles seven times, in triples three times, in RBI four times, and in slugging percentage six times. He finally retired at age forty-three, and later spent nineteen years as a Pirates coach.

More than just a great player, Wagner was a great sportsman. He played wherever and whenever he was needed, and never complained. Bill James wrote that, "he was a gentle, kind man, a storyteller, supportive of rookies, patient with fans, cheerful in hard times, careful of the example that he set for youth, a hard worker, a man who had no enemies and who never forgot his friends."[2]

In 1936, Honus Wagner became one of the first five players selected for the Baseball Hall of Fame. He wasn't quite the best hitter who ever lived, or the best base runner or fielder. But nobody could do all those things better than Honus, and nobody was a better team player. "There is no question that Wagner was the greatest all-around ballplayer who ever lived," said longtime baseball executive Ed Barrow. "He could have played any position and would have been a great star."[3]

HONUS WAGNER

BORN: February 24, 1874, Mansfield, Pennsylvania.

DIED: December 6, 1955, Carnegie, Pennsylvania.

PRO: Louisville Colonels, 1897–1899; Pittsburgh Pirates, 1900–1917.

RECORDS: Most years leading NL in batting average (8); Most triples, NL (252).

HONORS: Elected to National Baseball Hall of Fame, 1936.

Taking a mighty cut, Wagner is able to get around on the pitcher's offering. Wagner was the first player to have his name imprinted on his bats.

TED WILLIAMS

Ted Williams won his second Triple Crown in 1947. Rogers Hornsby is the only other player to win more than one Triple Crown.

TED WILLIAMS

TED WILLIAMS WAS FORTY-TWO years old and ready to retire after his last scheduled game at Boston's Fenway Park. It was a cool, gray day, and the air was heavy. A standing ovation greeted Williams' eighth-inning appearance, which the fans realized would probably be his last. They hoped he could finish his career with a base hit.

Williams turned on a fastball and sent it 420 feet toward right center field. "The ball kept going and going into the jowls of that strong wind," recalled a Boston executive, "and it finally made the bullpen."[1] After the game, Williams said, "I am convinced I've quit at the right time. There's nothing more I can do than hit a farewell home run."[2]

Theodore Samuel Williams was born in San Diego, California, on August 30, 1918. He attended Herbert Hoover High School, and grew up on the playgrounds of San Diego. Tall and skinny, the left-handed pull hitter had quick wrists and uncanny eyesight. He signed his first pro contract right after graduation.

By age twenty, Williams was an outfielder on the Red Sox. He studied and practiced hitting day and night. "All I want out of life," said the confident youngster, "is that when I walk down the street folks will say 'there goes the greatest hitter who ever lived.'"[3] Williams went on to lead the AL with 145 RBI, a rookie record.

Two years later, Williams had one of the best seasons of all time. He led the AL in home runs, runs scored, walks, on-base percentage (.551), slugging (.735), and batting (.406). In more than half a century since then, no other major-leaguer has topped the .400 barrier. For an encore,

Williams won the Triple Crown in 1942. He was named the Major League Player of the Year in both seasons.

Williams' soaring career then was put on hold for three years. The United States was involved in World War II, and Williams enlisted in the Naval Air Corps. He returned in time for the 1946 season.

Williams picked up right where he left off. He led Boston to the AL pennant, and was named the league's MVP. A year later, he won his second Triple Crown and his third Player of the Year Award. In 1948, he led the AL with a .369 average, and in 1949, he was named MVP and Player of the Year after setting career highs with 43 homers and 159 RBI.

A second stint in military service kept Ted out of baseball for most of the 1952 and 1953 seasons. Various physical problems, including a broken elbow, broken collarbone, and a neck injury, also cost him a great deal of playing time during the 1950s. Nothing could stop him from hitting, however. In 1957, at age thirty-nine, he batted an incredible .388, earning his record fifth Player of the Year citation.

Williams finally retired with 521 home runs and a .344 career batting average. His .634 lifetime slugging percentage ranks second all-time, and his .483 on-base percentage is the best ever. If not for the nearly five seasons he missed in military service, Williams might have hit close to 700 career homers and set all-time records for runs scored, RBI, and walks. All in all, Ted Williams became just what he set out to be: "the greatest hitter who ever lived."

TED WILLIAMS

BORN: August 30, 1918, San Diego, California.

HIGH SCHOOL: Herbert Hoover High School, San Diego, California.

PRO: Boston Red Sox, 1939–1942, 1946–1960.

RECORDS: Highest on-base percentage, season (.551 in 1941) and career (.483).

HONORS: Triple Crown, 1942, 1947; AL MVP, 1946, 1949; Major League Player of the Year, 1941, 1942, 1947, 1949, 1957; Major League Player of the Decade, 1960; Elected to National Baseball Hall of Fame, 1966.

Despite missing most of five seasons due to military service, Williams compiled some of the best statistics ever. He ranks in the top fifteen in most major offensive categories.

CHAPTER NOTES

Hank Aaron

1. Wayne Minshew, "Hank's 3,000-Hit Dream Born in '54," *The Sporting News*, May 23, 1970, p. 3.

2. Atlanta Braves 400 Club and Atlanta Chamber of Commerce, "Quotes About Hank Aaron," *Atlanta Salutes Hank Aaron* (1974), p. 3.

Ty Cobb

1. H. G. Salsinger, "Cobb or Ruth—Which was Tops?," *The Sporting News*, May 24, 1950, p. 3.

2. Bob Broeg, *SuperStars of Baseball* (South Bend, Ind.: Diamond Communications, 1994), p. 67.

3. Sid Keener, "Scribe-Pal Goes to Bat for Cobb," *The Sporting News*, December 27, 1961, p. 11.

Tony Gwynn

1. Peter Richmond, "Trouble in Paradise," *The National Sports Daily*, June 25, 1990, p. 38.

2. Phil Collier, "Gwynn Boosted for Bat Crown," *The Sporting News*, July 2, 1984, p. 24.

Rogers Hornsby

1. John Drebinger, "The Retroactive Award for .424 in '24—The Rajah," *BBWAA Scorebook* no. 1, 1962; "Rogers Hornsby" biographical file, National Baseball Library and Archive.

2. Steve Gietschier, "The Batter's Box Was His World," *The Sporting News*, September 4, 1995, p. 9.

3. Associated Press, "Hornsby Elected to Hall of Fame" (January 20, 1942); "Rogers Hornsby" biographical file, National Baseball Library & Archive.

Stan Musial

1. Joe Reichler, "Musial Story: Stan Rises to $650 a Game," *St. Louis Globe-Democrat*, February 23, 1958; "Stanley F. Musial" biographical file, National Baseball Library and Archive.

2. Cliff Evans, "So They Tell Me," *The Sporting News*, March 23, 1963, p. 32.

Pete Rose
1. Gary Stein, "Rose Already Paying Dividends," *Poughkeepsie Journal*, May 16, 1979, p. 27.
2. Pete Rose with Hal Bodley, *Countdown to Cobb* (St. Louis: The Sporting News, 1985), p. 210.

Babe Ruth
1. Bert Randolph Sugar, *The Book of Sports Quotes* (New York: Quick Fox, 1979), p. 34.

Frank Thomas
1. Rick Gano, "Big Hurt Putting Dent in Record Books," *Albany Times Union*, March 26, 1996, p. D6.

Honus Wagner
1. Honus Wagner as told to Les Biederman, "Circling the Bases with the Flying Dutchman," *The Sporting News*, November 22, 1950, p. 13.
2. Bill James, *The Bill James Historical Baseball Abstract* (New York: Villard Books, 1986), p. 372.
3. "Honus Wagner Dies; 'Old Bowlegs' Called Baseball's Greatest," *Pittsburgh Press*, December 6, 1955, p. 2.

Ted Williams
1. Fred Ciampa, "Step by Step Through the Career of Ted Williams," *Boston Record American*, April 23, 1969, p. A6.
2. Phil Spartano, "Cooperstown Ready to Welcome a Giant," *Utica Observer-Dispatch*, January 28, 1966; "Theodore S. Williams" biographical file, National Baseball Library and Archive.
3. John Updike, "Hub Fans Bid Kid Adieu," *The New Yorker*, October 22, 1960; "Theodore S. Williams" biographical file, National Baseball Library and Archive.

INDEX